A New True Book

GHANA

By Karen Jacobsen

Flag of Ghana

CHILDRENS PRESS ®

CHICAGO

JUL 1994

Each bus has its own name in Accra,
the capital city of Ghana.

PHOTO CREDITS

AP/Wide World Photos—27, 28, 30

Bruce Coleman Incorporated—13 (left);
© Norman Myers, 9

© John Elk III—Cover,
18, 19 (right), 20 (2 photos), 25 (right), 41
(left), 43 (right), 45 (2 photos)

Reprinted with permission of *The New Book
of Knowledge*, 1991 edition, © Grolier, Inc.—
5

Historical Pictures Service—25 (left)

© David G. Houser—13 (right), 22, 35

© Hutchinson Library—10; © Ann Tully, 33

Odyssey/Frerck/Chicago—© Robert Frerck,
17 (right), 19 (left), 42 (2 photos), 43 (left),
44 (right)

Photo Researchers, Inc.—© John Moss, 17
(left)

Photri—39

Root Resources—© Mary Albright, 14; © Ted
Farrington, 15 (left)

Tom Stack & Associates—© Janet M.
Milhomme, 40

SuperStock International, Inc.—6, 7

TSW-CLICK/Chicago—© Brian Seed, 2, 8
(right), 12, 37

Valan—© Brian Atkinson, 8 (left), 41 (right),
44 (left); © Aubrey Lang, 15 (top right); © Jim
Merli, 15 (bottom right)

Courtesy Flag Research Center,
Winchester, Massachusetts 01890—
Cover inset: Flag of Ghana

Cover—Elmina market people

Library of Congress Cataloging-in-Publication Data

Jacobsen, Karen.
  Ghana / by Karen Jacobsen.
    p.   cm. — (A New true book)
  Includes index.
  Summary: Explores the geography, history, people,
and culture of Ghana.
  ISBN 0-516-01135-9
  1. Ghana—Juvenile literature.   [1.   Ghana.]
I. Title.
QT510.J32   1992
966.7—dc20   91-35273
                                          CIP
                                           AC

TABLE OF CONTENTS

THE NATION

Ghana is in western Africa. Three countries share borders with Ghana– Ivory Coast in the west, Burkina Faso in the north, and Togo in the east. The Gulf of Guinea forms Ghana's southern border. Beyond the gulf is the Atlantic Ocean.

Ghana lies just north of the equator. Along the coast, the climate is hot and damp.

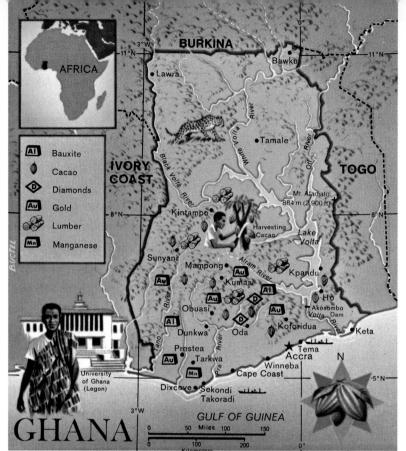

Ghana is shaped like a rectangle. It is 445 miles from north to south and 310 miles from west to east.

Inland, the climate is hot and very dry.

Ghana used to be called the Gold Coast. But when the Gold Coast became independent in

1957, it changed its name to Ghana. The name comes from the old Ghana Empire that ruled in western Africa from A.D. 300 to 1200.

Accra is the capital city of Ghana. Almost one million people live in Accra.

Street markets in Accra, the capital city of Ghana

The harbor at Tema has modern docks and machinery to unload cargo ships.

THE LAND

Heavy surf pounds much of Ghana's coast. The waters are dangerous, and there are no natural harbors.. But about thirty years ago, a safe harbor was built at Tema— a city east of Accra.

7

Vegetables for sale on a street in Accra (left). In northern
Ghana, people build round houses with grass roofs.

The land along the
coast of Ghana is flat. The
soil is rich and there is
plenty of rain. Farmers in
southern Ghana are able
to grow many crops, such
as bananas, coffee, sugar,
corn, cassava, and peanuts.

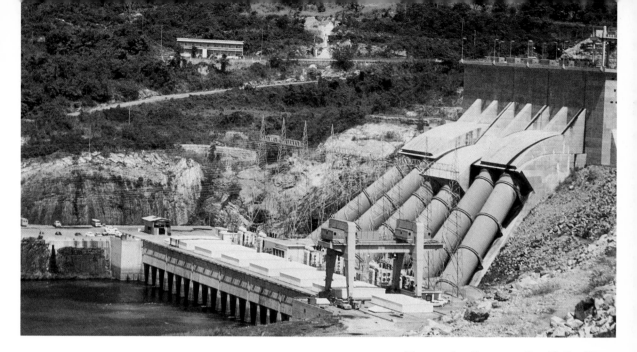

Akosombo Dam on the Volta River

Lake Volta covers much of eastern Ghana. The lake was created in 1966 when the Akosombo Dam was built. The dam created electric power for many parts of Ghana.

South of the dam, the Volta River passes through

the Akwapim-Togo Hills on its way to the Gulf of Guinea. Mount Afadjato, near the Togo border, rises 2,905 feet.

A large tropical forest lies south of the Kwahu Plateau in west central Ghana. The forest provides mahogany, ebony, and other valuable trees for lumber. In the shade of the forest's tall trees, farmers grow cacao, Ghana's most important crop.

The ripe cacao pods are cut open with sharp knives. The beans inside are shelled, dried, and ground into powder to make chocolate.

Much of central and northern Ghana is savanna, a rolling plain of grass. There are few trees or bushes. In most years, little rain falls in the north during the summer months. But farmers are able to grow corn, yams, and peanuts. And ranchers raise cattle on the grasslands.

Cattle share their pasture with a flock of birds.

Lemurs (left) are found in Ghana's forests. Giraffes (above) live in the Mole Game Preserve.

WILDLIFE

Ghana's tropical forest is growing smaller. People cut down the trees for wood or to create farmland. Ghana has now set aside large pieces of land as national parks. By

Hippopotamuses like the mud and pools in the wet flatlands.

law, no one can cut down
trees or hunt animals
inside these parks.

Ghana's population of
large wild animals is also
much smaller. Hunters
killed elephants for their
ivory tusks. Lions and
other large cats were

Buffalo (above), crocodiles (top right), and snakes (right) live in Ghana. Insects carry diseases such as malaria and sleeping sickness.

driven away by farmers. But many buffalo, hippopotamuses, antelopes, and wild hogs, as well as monkeys, birds, and snakes still live in the forests and grasslands. Crocodiles swim in the rivers.

THE PEOPLE

Almost fifteen million people live in Ghana. A few thousand are Europeans or Asians. The rest—more than 99 percent—are Africans. They belong to several different tribes. Each tribe has its own language.

Nearly half of Ghana's people are Ashanti. They live mainly in the center of the country. Members of the Fanti tribe live near the coast. The Ga have villages in the central and

An Ashanti chief in ceremonial robes (left).
This Ga family (right) lives in Accra.

southern parts of the
country. The Ewe live east
of Lake Volta.

Ghana's fishermen fish from canoes. They catch
the fish with nets hauled in by hand.

LIVING IN GHANA

Many people live in small
fishing villages along the coast.
But most people in southern
Ghana live in small family
groups near their farmland.

Food is cooked outside
by several families

A woman making *fufu* (left). A pan of plantains, a kind of banana (right), cooking

together. A favorite food is *fufu*, made of boiled and mashed cassavas or yams. Fufu is rolled into balls and dipped into a thick soup or stew.

Most Ghanians wear Western-style clothing. But

Man wearing a *ntama* (left). Women wear *ntama* skirts and *kaba* blouses (right).

many men still wear long robes called *ntamas*. Women wear *ntamas* as skirts with blouses called *kabas*.

Cacao is Ghana's biggest money crop. It is sold all over the world. Rubber, palm oil, and kola nuts are also sold to other countries.

Ghana has several valuable natural resources. Miners dig up large amounts of gold. There are also manganese and bauxite mines. Manganese is a metal used in iron and copper alloys. Bauxite ore is the source of aluminum.

Diamonds are found near rivers. An oil field is being developed off Ghana's coast in the Gulf of Guinea.

Rivers and coastal lagoons are used for transportation.
Ancient stone tools have been found along the banks
of the White Volta River.

LONG AGO IN GHANA

Ghana's first people were hunters and gatherers. They lived on the grasslands and along the rivers.

About 800 years ago, Ashanti people arrived from northern and western Africa. They settled in the central forestlands at Kumasi. The Ashanti took control of a large area and set up their own kingdom.

THE EUROPEANS

The Portuguese were the first Europeans to sail along the coast of West Africa. In 1471 they came to Ghana and found that the people had huge amounts of gold.

The Portuguese built forts. They traded European goods for African gold. They named the land *Costa D'Oro*, which means "coast of gold" in Portuguese.

Other European traders–

English, French, Dutch, Swedes, Danes, and Germans—also built trading posts along the Gold Coast.

During the 1500s the Europeans were still trading for gold and ivory. They also began buying slaves to sell as workers in the Americas.

Drawing of a raid on a village on market day. The villagers captured during this raid might have been shipped to America and sold as slaves.

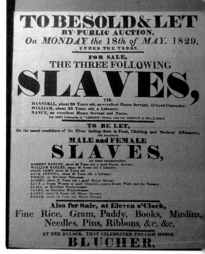

TO BE SOLD & LET
BY PUBLIC AUCTION,
On MONDAY the 18th of MAY. 1829,
UNDER THE TREES.
FOR SALE,
THE THREE FOLLOWING
SLAVES,
VIZ.
HANNIBAL, about 30 Years old, an excellent House Servant, of Good Character.
WILLIAM, about 35 Years old, a Labourer.
NANCY, an excellent House Servant and Nurse.
The MEN belonging to "LEECH'S" Estate, and the WOMAN to Mrs. D. SMIT.

TO BE LET,
On the usual conditions of the Hirer finding them in Food, Clothing, and Medical Allowance,
THE FOLLOWING
MALE and FEMALE
SLAVES,
42 IN NUMBER,
ROBERT BAGLEY, about 20 Years old, a good House Servant.
WILLIAM BAGLEY, about 27 Years old, a Labourer.
JOHN ARMS, about 18 Years old.
JACK ANTONIA, about 40 Years old, a Labourer.
PHILIP, an Excellent Fisherman.
HARRY, about 27 Years old, a good House Servant.
LUCY, a Young Woman of good Character, used to House Work and the Nursery.
ELIZA, an Excellent Washerwoman.
CLARA, an Excellent Washerwoman.
FANNY, about 14 Years old, House Servant.
SARAH, about 14 Years old, House Servant.

Also for Sale, at Eleven o'Clock,
Fine Rice, Gram, Paddy, Books, Muslins,
Needles, Pins, Ribbons, &c. &c.
AT ONE O'CLOCK, THAT CELEBRATED ENGLISH HORSE
BLUCHER,

GOLD COAST CROWN COLONY

Great Britain outlawed slavery in 1807. But the British still wanted African gold. By 1872, the Dutch, the Danes, and the other Europeans had left the Gold Coast. Only the British stayed. They tried to take complete control of the area.

But the Ashanti would not give up their land. In 1901, after many battles,

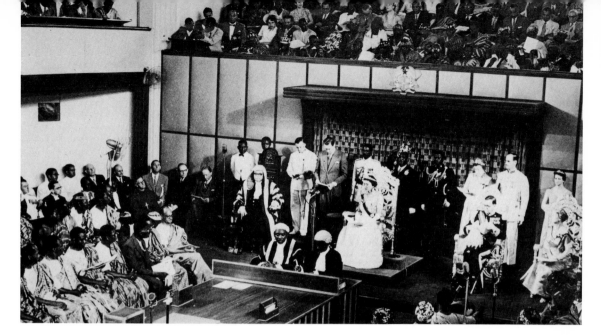

Representing the queen of Great Britain, the Dutchess of Kent met with Ghana's parliament on the day the Gold Coast colony became the independent country of Ghana.

the British army won. The British coastal land and the Ashanti kingdom were joined together as the Gold Coast Crown Colony of Great Britain.

Under British rule, the Africans were governed by British law.

At the end of World War II (1939-1945), a new constitution gave the people of Ghana more power in the government. But some African leaders wanted the end of British rule. They wanted complete independence.

Kwame Nkrumah (1909-1972) was the son of a goldsmith. He went to mission schools in the Gold Coast Crown Colony and to universities in the United States. In 1947, he came home to lead his country in its struggle for independence.

KWAME NKRUMAH

In 1949, Kwame Nkrumah (1909-1972) formed the Convention People's Party (CPP). Its motto was "Self-government now." Nkrumah and his supporters led strikes against the British colonial government. In 1950, he was put in jail for causing trouble.

A year later, there was an election, and the CPP candidates won. The British released Nkrumah

A crowd in Accra celebrates Ghana's independence on March 6, 1957.

from jail, and in 1952, he was elected the first prime minister of the Gold Coast. In 1957, the Gold Coast became the independent state of Ghana.

In 1960, Ghana became a republic. Kwame Nkrumah was elected president and the CPP was the nation's only political party.

Nkrumah became very powerful. But money was in short supply and there were many problems.

In February 1966, the army and police overthrew Nkrumah. The new leaders did away with the constitution and outlawed the CPP. The new head of government was General Joseph Ankrah. In 1969, he was replaced by Akwasi Amankwa Afrifa.

CHANGES IN GOVERNMENT

Since 1969, the government has changed many times. Presidents are elected and then thrown out by army officers.

In June 1979, Lieutenant Jerry Rawlings of the air force led another takeover. Rawlings' government executed Ghana's former leaders—Akwasi Amankwa Afrifa, Lieutenant Colonel Ignatius Kutu Acheampong,

Lieutenant Jerry Rawlings and his council took over the government of Ghana in 1981.

and General Frederick W. K. Akuffo.

New elections were held, and Dr. Hilla Limann became president. But in December 1981, Rawlings again overthrew the government. He did away with the constitution and the National Assembly. In their place, he set up the Provisional National Defense Council (PNDC). Rawlings made himself its chairman.

The 1980s brought many problems to Ghana. There were food shortages. People lost their jobs. Lake Volta began to dry up. Many Ghanians left home to work in Nigeria. But, in 1983, the Nigerian

The local people get water from a public well near the town of Bolgatanga.

government made more than a million Ghanians return to their homeland. The shortages of food, water, housing, and jobs became worse. Ghana has very little money to use to solve its problems.

EDUCATION

Most people in northern Ghana are Muslims. Their leaders teach boys how to read the Koran, the holy book of the Muslims.

In Ghana's cities and towns, children must go to school for at least ten years. Their education is free.

At age six, students start school. They study arithmetic, history, and

The government is trying to offer basic education to more children and to adults. Teachers go to small villages to teach basic subjects to young and old.

science. English is the official language in Ghana. So students also study in English.

After sixth grade, students go to junior secondary school for five years. Junior-level students study more advanced subjects. Because farming is so important in Ghana, students also learn how to grow food crops.

Good students may go on to attend upper-level secondary schools for another two years.

Ghana has three universities: the University of Ghana at Legon, the University of Science and Technology at Kumasi, and

At the University of Ghana, students study law, medicine, engineering, business, or other advanced subjects.

the University of Cape Coast.

Outside the cities, many children never have a chance to go to school. Only 30 percent of Ghana's people can read and write.

These children hope to be on one of Ghana's national teams.

SPORTS

Schoolchildren enjoy fast games. Boys like to play football (soccer).

Track-and-field sports are popular with both boys and girls. Ghanian athletes take part in international track-and-field events.

HOLIDAYS

About 43 percent of Ghana's people are Christians. They celebrate Christmas, Easter, and other Christian holidays. About 12 percent are Muslims. They celebrate the feasts and holy days of Islam. Many Ghanians

A Muslim mosque, or house of worship (below), and a Christian church (right)

Ga people in Accra celebrate at a harvest feast.

follow the old beliefs of
their tribes.

Everyone celebrates
Independence Day (March 6),
Republic Day (July 1),
and Revolution Day
(December 31).

A carved wooden mask (left). Stools (above) are very important to the Ashanti people. Fathers carve stools to give to their newborn babies. Bridegrooms carve stools as wedding gifts for their brides.

ARTS AND CRAFTS

The carving of wood and ivory is an important skill in Ghana. The Ashanti carve stools and beautiful statues. Other tribes carve wooden masks for use in ceremonies.

43

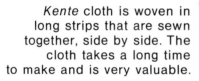

Kente cloth is woven in long strips that are sewn together, side by side. The cloth takes a long time to make and is very valuable.

Handwoven cloth, called *kente* cloth, is Ghana's most famous craft product. Its brightly colored patterns are woven by Ashanti men. Today, Ghana has many

problems. But it also has many rich resources. Its people are finding new ways to solve their problems—to make life better in their nation. In time, Ghana promises to become a leading nation in modern Africa.

WORDS YOU SHOULD KNOW

alloy (AL • loy) — a mixture of metals

assembly (uh • SEM • blee) — a group of elected people who make laws for a country

bauxite (BOX • ite) — a claylike ore that contains aluminum

cacao (kuh • KOW • o) — a small tree from whose seeds cocoa and chocolate are made

cassava (kuh • SAH • vah) — a plant with starchy roots used for food

colony (KAHL • uh • nee) — an area controlled or settled by people from another country

constitution (kahn • stih • TOO • shun) — a set of rules or laws for the government of a group of people

equator (ih • KWAY • ter) — an imaginary line around the Earth, equally distant from the North and South poles

execute (EX • ih • kyoot) — to put to death

harbor (HAR • bor) — a safe place on a seacoast for ships to land

independent (in • dih • PEN • dint) — free from the control of another country or person

international (in • ter • NASH • uh • nil) — between nations

ivory (EYE • vree) — a hard, white substance that makes up the tusks of some animals such as elephants

manganese (MAN • guh • neez) — a grayish metal used in alloys

minister (MIN • iss • ter) — an elected leader

ntama (n • TAH • mah) — a long cloth robe or skirt worn by the people of Ghana

outlaw (OWT • law) — to make unlawful; to pass a law against

republic (rih • PUB • lik) — a country with elected leaders who represent the people

resources (RE • sor • sez) — supplies of valuable natural materials such as metals or gems

savanna (suh • VAN • uh) — a broad grassland with few trees

shortage (SHOR • tij) — a lack of things that are needed, such as food or clothing

subject (SUB • ject) — a citizen of a country that has a king or queen

surf (SERF) — waves that break on a shore

tribe (TRYB) — a group of people related by blood and customs

tropical forest (TRAH • pih • kil FOR • ist) — a thick evergreen forest that grows in the tropics, where there is much rain

university (yoo • nih • VER • sih • tee) — a school of higher learning

yam (YAM) — the starchy root of a climbing plant

INDEX

About the Author

   Karen Jacobsen is a graduate of the University of Connecticut and Syracuse University. She has been a teacher and is a writer. She likes to find out about interesting subjects and then write about them.